IMAGES OF WAR
JOSEPH STALIN

IMAGES OF WAR
JOSEPH STALIN

NIGEL BLUNDELL

Pen & Sword
MILITARY

First published in Great Britain in 2017 by
PEN & SWORD MILITARY
an imprint of
Pen & Sword Books Ltd,
47 Church Street,
Barnsley,
South Yorkshire.
S70 2AS

A CIP record for this book is available from the British Library.

ISBN 978 1 52670 203 6

Typeset by Chic Media Ltd

Printed and bound by CPI UK

Pen & Sword Books Ltd incorporates the Imprints of
Pen & Sword Aviation, Pen & Sword Maritime, Pen & Sword Military, Pen & Sword Family History, Pen & Sword Discovery, Wharncliffe Local History, Wharncliffe True Crime, Wharncliffe Transport, Pen & Sword Select, Pen & Sword Military Classics, Leo Cooper, The Praetorian Press, Remember When, Seaforth Publishing and Frontline Publishing.

For a complete list of Pen & Sword titles please contact
Pen & Sword Books Limited
47 Church Street, Barnsley, South Yorkshire, S70 2AS, England
E-mail: enquiries@pen-and-sword.co.uk
Website: www.pen-and-sword.co.uk

Introduction

Who was Joseph Stalin? A political giant and leader of the vastest nation on earth, he was one of the most dominant figures of the twentieth century. He was a revolutionary, an astute politician, a global power broker, a crowd-pulling idol with plenipotentiary power over 200 million people.

He was also a monster. He sacrificed his friends and allies in pursuit of power, murdered thousands of his rivals with sadistic brutality and callously obliterated millions more of his own citizens during the quarter century of his leadership.

His life was one of contradictions. He was the son of serfs yet clawed his way to power over the heads of intellectuals, politicians and statesmen. He espoused great ideals yet he was a boorish bully. He was heralded as a great victor yet his ineptitude lost him entire armies. He championed the cause of the masses yet delivered them into mass graves.

This, then, was the astonishingly paradoxical figure of Joseph Stalin, a name he adopted in his mid-Thirties. Stalin is from the Russian for 'Man of Steel'. A better title might have been 'Man of Blood'. For apart from being a war leader who sacrificed his own forces in millions, he was arguably the most destructive human being of his age.

His fellow monster of the twentieth century, Adolf Hitler, is often referred to as the world's worst mass murderer. But although millions died at Hitler's behest, Stalin was responsible for even more senseless deaths. At least eight million people were killed while this granite-faced tyrant ruled the Soviet Union. Millions more died as a direct result of his ideologically inspired policies.

Stalin's motives were confused: a deadly brew of revenge, ambition, fear and bloodlust. He liked to watch the interrogation of political suspects by his secret police and ordered them to 'beat, beat and beat again until they come crawling to you on their bellies with confessions in their teeth'. It is astonishing to think that those words were uttered by an international statesman and world leader who sat with giants like Churchill and Roosevelt and who single-handedly changed the course of history for many dangerous decades.

Almost as frightening as the horrendous crimes that Stalin committed is the level of idolatry that allowed this ogre to flourish. Just like Hitler, Stalin saw himself as a master of destiny, a role that excused the vilest atrocities. And, bafflingly, just like his Nazi counterpart, he was allowed to dominate his nation and overrun others with the enthusiastic support of the majority of the citizens whom he had subjugated.

Avuncular image of 'Uncle Joe', saviour of his people … but in reality a monstrous mass murderer.

Stalin was lauded as a national saviour right up until his death, which was marked by mourning crowds so vast that untold numbers perished in the crush.

This unquestioning adulation is not only a mystery to today's historians but a cause for alarm. For, under the Soviet Union's present regime, there are signs that the Stalin cult is being resurrected as the Russian bear again sharpens its claws.

That is why this book implicitly contains a warning from history. The concise life story that follows hopefully presents a cautionary picture, in words and historic photographs, of the son of serfs who, destined for the priesthood, instead became a street-fighting revolutionary using torture and terror as tools to attain power.

It poses the mystery of how the brutish drunkard he became could nevertheless have been lauded abroad as a cultural giant and could, in his own country, have spellbound so many millions as an object of worship.

It aims to provide clues as to how Stalin the military incompetent came to be seen as a statesman of equal standing to war leaders like Churchill and Hitler (whose lives are similarly covered by companion volumes in the Pen & Sword 'Images of War' series).

And it points to the danger of rewriting history to allow the resurrection of the monster Stalin as a 'father' of his people in the twenty-first century. For the despot who forged the Iron Curtain and whose personality cult attained Messianic proportions should be recognised not as a self-styled towering 'Man of Steel' but as a bloodstained, mere 5ft 5ins tall idol with feet of clay.

Nothing about the life and character of Joseph Stalin was straightforward – not even his name and the date of his birth. The man who would one day rule the vastest country on earth was born in the winter of 1879 in a small poverty-stricken enclave of Georgia, which was then part of the Russian Empire. His birth name in Georgian was Ioseb Besarionis dze Jughashvili, the Russian version of which was the almost equally tongue-twisting Vissarionovich Dzhugashvili. As was customary, he later adopted a string of briefer nicknames, mostly chosen to glamourise his wayward youth, his favourite being 'Koba' (meaning 'the indomitable') after the Robin Hood-like hero of a popular novel. He did not use the tile Joseph Stalin (translated by him as 'Man of Steel') until he was in his thirties.

Stalin's nomenclature is muddled enough but even his date of birth has been a cause of confusion. Throughout his years in power, he had it recorded as 21 December 1879, as published in his official biography and the day on which nationwide celebrations took place. Only after the collapse of the Soviet Union was it revealed in baptismal records that the real date of his birth was three days earlier, on 18 December.

On that dark wintry day, the lusty cries of the newborn infant told his mother Ekaterina Dzhugashvili all she needed to know: that he was a strong, healthy child, perfect except that the second and third toes of his left foot were joined together. With his safe arrival in the world, her dearest wish had come true. This was her fourth pregnancy yet none of the other babies had lived. She resolved that Iosif Vissarionovich would grow up to be a priest by way of thanks to God.

Home was little more than a shack in Gori, a small town 60 kilometres from the Georgian capital Tblisi (then known as Tiflis). There was one room only and the few sticks of furniture in it were simply crafted out of wood. Stalin's hovel still exists today, dwarfed by a marble mock-temple built to honour the birthplace during his era in power.

Ekaterina, or 'Keke' as she was better known, was determined that her adored only son would escape the grinding poverty she had known all her life. To this end, she slaved as a washerwoman and at other menial labours, saving enough money to buy him an education. She was poor and illiterate but even she could see that this was the only possible means of liberation from a dire existence.

Her boundless motherly love of little Iosif, whom she nick-named Soso, was beyond question but didn't prevent her from meting out beatings to her mischievous son. However, the swipes he suffered from her were nothing compared to the thrashings he endured from his father.

Vissarion Djugashvili inflicted vicious punishment on his only son, much of it apparently carried out for the sheer pleasure it gave him. Vissarion was a cobbler but he sacrificed his skills in favour of heavy drinking. In addition to the brutal beatings

Stalin was born on 18 December 1879 in a tiny flat rented by his parents in this house in Gori, Georgia.

A sketch and photograph of Stalin's mother Ekaterina Geladze, wife of Vissarion Dzhugashvili. He was a bootmaker and she a washerwoman.

he took himself, the young Stalin witnessed his loutish father attack his beloved mother. Yet Keke was no wilting flower. Although slight and pale, she lashed out at her errant husband many times while they lived together. It was during one such bout of violence between the couple that an outraged Stalin grabbed a kitchen knife and hurled it at Vissarion. Stalin instantly ran off and sought refuge from his father's wrath with a neighbour.

When times got hard, Vissarion took a job in a boot factory away from home, although he returned periodically to terrorise his wife and son. When he died in a drunken brawl in 1890, he was something of a tramp. His passing was nothing short of a blessed relief for Stalin.

If poverty and abuse were not enough to contend with, Stalin had other disadvantages in childhood. An attack of smallpox which almost killed him left him severely pock-marked. The scars were so deep that photographs taken of him much later were doctored to disguise the disfigurement. In addition, his left arm was shorter than his right by four inches, possibly due to an accident in which he was run over by a carriage while watching a religious festival.

Stalin was not going to let any of this stand in his way. The traumas of childhood did not make him withdrawn, as is often the case. When he began school in September 1888, rather than being bullied, he was himself the aggressor.

Schoolmates have testified that the young Stalin was awestruck by the wild and spectacular terrain of Georgia, although he had no particular respect for the wildlife within it. He frequently passed the time by hurling stones at birds.

But there was a softer side to the boy. He loved books and sought out classic adventure stories that were banned in the classroom. Revealing an artistic nature, he loved to sketch. He sang in the church choir and was praised for his melodic tenor tones. He also impressed his teachers by his remarkable memory, being able to recite large chunks of the Bible. These were, however, qualities he largely suppressed long before he reached power for fear they were regarded as weaknesses or indulgences. What was also left unmentioned was that the future leader of Russia, who never lost his strong Georgian accent, only learned to speak Russian at the age of nine.

Following a six-year spell at the Gori church school, in 1894 Stalin graduated two years ahead and was awarded a scholarship to the Orthodox Theological Seminary in Tiflis to embark on the training his mother always vowed he would have. He was a boarder which meant that he was exposed to the harsh regime of the seminary around the clock. The studies were demanding and Stalin accrued a working knowledge of classical languages as well as Orthodox theology. He also devoured a wide range of books on subjects banned by the seminary, often getting himself into trouble in the process. Stalin was by now schooled far beyond the dreams of most Georgian boys.

Two early images of the schoolboy Vissarionovich Dzhugashvili, later known as Josef Stalin.

In 1898 Stalin took the pseudonym Koba and joined a Marxist study circle among railway workers meeting in this house in Tiflis.

A pre-Revolution photograph of the town of Tiflis (later Tbilisi).

It was while he was preparing for the priesthood in this repressive environment that Stalin got his first taste for the politics of change. Seminaries, top heavy with regulations and renowned for the cruelty of their masters, were paradoxically popular breeding grounds for revolutionaries. Secret meetings were held to discuss the theories of Marxism and to debate the need for revolution. By 1898 Stalin was a member of a local Georgian Marxist organisation called *Mesame Dasi* or Group Three. His behaviour worsened. He refused to work and was rude to the monks who tried to teach him. The following year, he left the seminary; if he was not expelled, he most certainly departed under a cloud. It was a move his mother regretted for the rest of her days — even when her son held sway over the entire Russian empire.

* * *

By the turn of the century Russia was on the verge of revolutionary turmoil. Terrorist assassination of high-ranking civil servants was chronic. Trades unions, officially banned, were nevertheless demanding better pay and conditions for the country's extremely impoverished industrial workers. The peasants had experienced a famine in 1897. There was no parliament in which grievances could be vented. The secret police, the Okhrana, were able to make arbitrary arrests and imprison people without trial.

Stalin had by now realised that Russia was ripe for revolution. The country's monarch had not foreseen it — but was to learn his lesson the hard way. Tsar Nicholas II had come to the throne in 1896, confessing to his future brother-in-law Grand Duke Alexander: 'I am not prepared to be a tsar. I never wanted to be one. I know nothing of the business of ruling.'

Tsar Nicholas was married to a German princess, Alexandra Feodorovna of Hesse-Darmstadt, a grandchild of Britain's Queen Victoria. This handsome, imperious woman was an unpopular figure but worshipped by her husband and, within the walls of their palaces, the couple were idyllically happy. They had four daughters and then a son, Alexei. Their joy at the birth of the heir to the Russian throne soon turned to dismay when they realised he suffered from haemophilia. The condition, inherent in the royal families of Europe, was a disabling one. Every bump or scratch would gush with blood and even the most experienced medic had difficulty in stemming the flow. The Tsar and his Tsarina focussed their energies on the survival of their only son, at the expense of the survival of the Russian empire.

The writing was on the wall long before the revolution of 1917. In January 1905 there was an uprising in which aggrieved St Petersburg peasants marched on the Winter Palace to present a petition to the Tsar, whom they termed their 'Little Father'. They were led by a priest and supposed trade union activist who was secretly on the police payroll. The Tsar's officials refused to acknowledge that the peasants' pitiful wages and appalling living conditions had fuelled a warranted desire for change. The reply dispatched to the protesters was an order to the army to open fire – and 200 men, women and children were killed, in an incident branded 'Bloody Sunday'.

A further 200 people were killed in April 1912 when soldiers opened fire on 5,000 men, women and children marching at the Lena goldfield in Siberia in protest at their starvation wages. Strikes and subversion became commonplace. The continuing harsh response of the army and the Okhrana showed a blatant disregard for human rights or life in their treatment of protesters.

It was this potent combination that turned peaceable Russian workers into hard-bitten revolutionaries. Russia was catapulting headlong into the industrial age, putting its vast powerhouse of natural resources to good use. The mines of Siberia, the oilfields of Azerbaijan and the crops of the Russian Steppes gave the empire a leg-up into the industrialised world. Yet the profits went into but few pockets. Those who toiled underground in the mines or braved the smog of the smoking oil wells were still hungry and clad in rags.

Against this grim background came World War I, with ill-equipped Russian soldiers pitted against the Kaiser's well-oiled war machine. The result was predictable. Russians were slaughtered or taken prisoner in their masses. Peasants were rounded up in the Russian countryside to take the place of those who had fallen at the front line. As the losses mounted, so did the bitterness of the working people, who knew full well that they were only being used as cannon fodder.

By September 1915 Tsar Nicholas was concerned enough about the conduct of his army in battle to leave the palace and head for the front line to command the troops personally. His actions were well intentioned but entirely foolhardy. The catastrophes of the battlefield were soon held to be his personal responsibility.

At home, meanwhile, Alexandra had fallen under the spell of a grubby, lecherous monk named Rasputin. The Tsarina appeared little more than a puppet to the conniving monk, whom she took to her heart because of his apparent power to heal the sickly Tsarevich Alexei. Rasputin had many supporters who believed he was gifted but others thought him a malevolent force who was making the royal couple look like idiots. On 29 December 1916 a group of noblemen took matters into their own hands by poisoning, shooting and then battering the raging Rasputin, who refused to die. When they finally disposed of his body in a freezing river, it is thought he was still alive. But the damage had been done. The authority of Russia's royal rulers had been shattered, and it was only months before the Tsarist regime was toppled for good.

Stalin, after leaving the Tiflis seminary, channelled all his energies towards the coming revolution. From the turn of the century, the revolutionary movement had spread its tentacles across the empire. Stalin concentrated his efforts in Georgia. In December 1899 he found a job as a clerk at the Tiflis Physical Observatory. He enjoyed free lodgings and a wage of 20 roubles a month. This is perhaps the only employment Stalin held down in his life, and his time in the post was short-lived. By May 1901 the police had raided the Observatory in a crackdown on subversives. Although Stalin escaped arrest, he deemed it impossible to return to his workplace. He thought it only a matter of time before he would be incarcerated like so many of his contemporaries. His only choice to avoid detention was to go underground.

Now he lived life as a rebel on a police 'wanted' list. He was one of a number who passed their days writing and printing revolutionary newspapers and pamphlets. By night there were meetings, some stormy and uproarious, all held in secret. He and others would graduate to robbery and thuggery to find more money for the movement during the years before the 1917 revolution.

The shadowy figure of the agitator Stalin was behind a May Day March in Tiflis in 1901 during which 14 people were wounded and more than 50 arrested. Once again, Stalin slipped through the clutches of the police and soldiers who went into action that day. On 9 March 1902 Stalin helped lead a demonstration at Batum. This time the troops opened fire, killing 15 and injuring 54 more.

The youthful Stalin is depicted at his most handsome. These may have been police photographs that were later heavily retouched for use as propaganda images.

By now Stalin was a member of a revolutionary committee. He was not popular, plaguing his fellow members with his arrogant brand of badgering. For Stalin was no democrat. He believed wholeheartedly in the extremes of the revolution. Anyone with views that differed, if only slightly, to his own, he would dismiss rudely, with ferocious hectoring. The meetings must have been noisy ones. The militants in the movement, the Bolsheviks (meaning 'belonging to the majority'), were beginning a bitter divorce from the more moderate Mensheviks ('menshe' meaning 'lesser').

The secret police finally caught up with Stalin in April 1902. He was held until July 1903, when he was exiled without trial to Siberia, thousands of miles from his home. Within seven months he escaped, with apparent ease, to continue his illicit activities.

The history of the Georgian revolutionary is intriguingly vague at this time, much of his youthful past having later been disguised or fictionalised. There is still little known about his romance and first marriage in 1906 – a tragic partnership that coloured his view on life and a subject that will be returned to later in the book.

There is also mystery around rumours that Stalin acted as a spy for the secret police during the early 1900s. Certainly his good fortune at slipping through the fingers of the police time and again seemed to some to be more than just luck. Others even doubted that he was sent to Siberia at all. After all, if he was not in the pay of the police, how was he supporting himself without work?

There have been many vain attempts to prove that self-seeker Stalin was in those days a traitor to his cause. But there is little doubt that he did betray an Armenian Bolshevik, Stepan Shaumyan, to the police in 1905. Shaumyan did not favour the heavy-handed, downright violent tactics advocated by Stalin but preferred a political advance of the revolutionary cause. His reasoned arguments swayed many and the rivalry between him and Stalin escalated – until Shaumyan was suddenly arrested at his secret hideaway. It was an address known only to Stalin.

Stalin was no more than a bit-part player during the unrest of 1905. At the end of that year, he attended a conference in Finland and met the man whose works had become his 'bible': Vladimir Ilyich Lenin. His first impressions of the revolutionary master were

Stepan Shaumyan was a fellow Bolshevik whom Stalin betrayed to the police in 1905.

contradictory. Here was the man to whom everybody deferred, yet he displayed none of the pomposity, posturing or obvious fervour that were the trademarks of his ilk. Lenin cut a distinctively unimpressive figure, plainly clad and quietly spoken.

Stalin was at first bemused by this modesty: 'I had hoped to see the mountain eagle of our party, the great man, great physically as well as politically. How great was my disappointment to see a most ordinary looking man.'

Stalin, however, quickly realised that the very presence of Lenin was enough to make people sit up and listen. It was a lesson in understatement that Stalin put to good use in later life – and was all the more menacing because of it. For his part, Lenin viewed Stalin as a loyal, talented Bolshevik worth watching and encouraging.

Stalin was temporarily exiled once more in September 1908 following his arrest in March of that year. No doubt rankled by the insolent, cocky young man, police seized him once again in March 1910. There followed spells in jail and months of freedom, in which Stalin played a cat-and-mouse game with the authorities. The internments gave him a new political

In December 1905 Stalin attended a Bolshevik conference in Finland, where he met his hero Vladimir Lenin – and was initially disappointed that he was 'in no way different from ordinary mortals'.

gravitas and he was promoted within the revolutionary movement from his Georgian realm to centre-stage at St Petersburg.

The end of his many periods of exile came in 1916 when he was told to leave his assigned home near the Arctic Circle to be assessed for military service. Despite later artistic portrayals of him at that age, he was no great physical example. Even disregarding his pockmarked face, Stalin's diminutive height of only 5ft 3ins, his bad teeth from years of exile and his foreshortened semi-disabled left arm meant he was rejected for formal soldiering. But the call to action would come from elsewhere, for the country was on the brink of revolution.

*   *   *

Police mugshots of Stalin, probably taken in 1910.

Looking cheerful despite being in exile in 1911… and, with beard, probably also taken while in exile.

Fearful that he was planning to escape from exile, the authorities ordered Stalin to be moved to the remote hamlet of Kureika on the Arctic Circle, where the temperature sometimes fell to 60F degrees below zero.

Stalin (back row in black hat) among a group of exiles in Monastyrskoe, Siberia, in 1914.

Ready for the 'class war' to come, Stalin in the uniform of the young revolutionary.

Stalin played a comparatively inconspicuous role in the early revolutionary movement although he did address a number of meetings, as later portrayed in this romanticised painting.

The overthrow of the Tsarist monarchy in March 1917 came as a breath of fresh air for most Russian citizens. Under the democratic Provisional Government, they could at last consort with whom they pleased, pronounce their opinions freely and read the books and newspapers of their choice. People naturally felt freed from a repressive regime. But after the October Revolution and the civil war that was to follow, when the Bolsheviks took charge, it would be years before they were free again.

Immediately following the overthrow of the royal establishment there was predictable chaos. Age-old systems of policing and government were dismantled but there was nothing to put in their place. The Provisional Government flailed helplessly in the face of national disarray. It persevered with an unpopular war with Germany that Russia was losing. Civil unrest escalated. Among the prime agitators were the Bolsheviks who, with a membership of some 40,000, were ready and willing to seize power.

When Lenin arrived in Russia from exile in Finland in October, he declared: 'History will not forgive us if we do not take power now.' His order for revolution finally came, scrawled in a child's notebook. The date was 25 October by the outdated Julian calendar used in Russia or 7 November by the Gregorian calendar prevalent in the rest of Europe.

Key communication points such as railway stations and telephone exchanges were occupied by Bolshevik troops in the early hours. By dawn the national bank was under siege. The Winter Palace, the seat of the Provisional Government, was stormed and its members arrested. Lenin proclaimed a new government and the Congress of Soviets met to endorse his action. The Bolshevik Revolution was now a fact – a world-changing Red coup that had thus far been achieved with comparatively few fatalities.

The Bolsheviks and their left-wing allies wanted an end to Russia's participation in World War One and achieved this with the peace pact known as the Brest-Litovsk Treaty signed in March 1918 between the new Soviet Russia and the Central Powers (Germany, Austria-Hungary, Bulgaria, and the Ottoman Empire). The Russian empire was dismembered by the treaty, with Ukraine, Finland, Poland and the Baltic states given their liberty and part of Belarus ceded to Germany.

However, there was no end in sight to the bloodshed. Armed forces loyal to the Tsar, known as 'White Russians', were still in the field. Foreign soldiers, including British, American, Japanese and French, arrived to back the 'Whites'. There were also troops who still supported the fallen Provisional Government ousted by the Red coup. In addition, there were resident foreign workers and prisoners of war, including 40,000 Czechs eager to return home and prepared to fight if necessary, not to mention a potent force of anarchists who would take on all-comers. It was a recipe for bloody civil war.

Born to power and privilege… the Russian royals on a visit to Balmoral Castle, Scotland, in 1896. Tsar Nicholas II stands behind Tsarina Alexandra, holding Grand Duchess Tatiana. The child's great-grandmother Queen Victoria is accompanied by her son the Prince of Wales, later King Edward VII.

Tsarina Alexandra fell under the spell of 'mad monk' Rasputin.

The resultant melee might easily have destabilised the minority supported Bolshevik government but Lenin was determined to rule with an iron fist. His lieutenant, Defence Minister Leon Trotsky, wielded fierce discipline to build and control an army of some five million. He used the death penalty liberally and, when troops had been disloyal, ordered that every tenth man should be shot.

The imperial Romanof family had remained under guard since Tsar Nicholas II's enforced abdication in March 1917. They had been offered asylum by Britain but were not allowed to leave Russia, instead being kept under house arrest, the new regime being nervous that the family could be used as a damaging rallying point for loyalists.

In the early hours of 17 July 1918 the family were awoken by their Bolshevik guards at the requisitioned merchant's house that served as their prison at Ekaterinburg, east of the Ural Mountains. The Tsar was told that anti-revolutionary forces were approaching the town and that orders had come from Moscow to move their entire entourage. The royal family and their servants were taken to a cellar and told to await transport to a more secure area. The guards had until two weeks earlier been peasant soldiers and, while not overly familiar, neither were they unfriendly. However, on 4 July they had been replaced by secret police under the command of fanatical revolutionary Yacov Yurovsky. And his men were not gaolers, they were executioners.

The Tsar and his household gathered in the dingy cellar, with a heavy iron grill protecting its only window, and waited for the transport that never came. Instead Yurovsky and his men entered and informed them that they were to be shot. As the Tsar rose to protest, Yurovsky fired a bullet into his head. A fusillade cut down the Tsarina and three of her daughters, along with two servants and the family doctor. The soldiers then turned their bayonets on the other adults still standing. The Tsar's son, Alexis, had been wounded and when he stirred was stamped to death by the soldiers. Yurovsky administered the coup de grace, placing his pistol to the boy's ear and firing two shots. Even the family's pet dog had its skull smashed in by a rifle butt. The bodies were bundled into lorries and driven to a mineshaft where they were mutilated and buried. They did not remain there long, however, because the White Army was counter-attacking in the area. So a day or two later, the remains of the imperial Romanov dynasty were irreverently removed to a secret resting place deep in the neighbouring forest.

The assassination was an unnecessarily brutal act that reverberated around the globe. This kind of savagery became a hallmark of the Bolshevik regime, although the atrocities of the civil war were by no means the preserve of the Reds alone, the Whites being equally guilty of inhuman outrages.

Extraordinarily, fashionable women flocked to meet the lecherous monk Rasputin, whose supporters believed was a gifted healer.

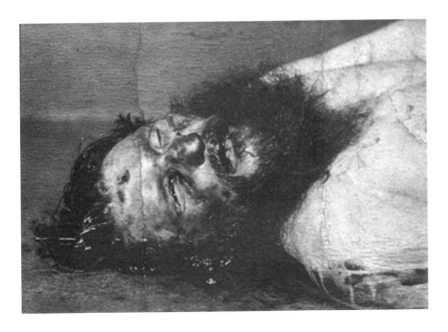

In order to end his malevolent influence over the Romanov royal family, in 1916 a group of noblemen killed Rasputin by poisoning him, battering him, shooting him and throwing him into a freezing river.

Tsar Nicholas II and his family in 1914. Under house arrest since his enforced abdication in 1917, the Romanovs were ushered into a cellar on 17 July 1918 and massacred by Red Guards.

Stalin revelled in the violence and gloried in the burgeoning power of the Bolsheviks. He liked to present himself as a man of action but he also became intoxicated by the expanding bureaucracy that was establishing itself. Officially, his role was People's Commissar for Nationalities, which dealt with the nation's non-Russian peoples, but his brief was far broader. He began by travelling the country to mobilise support. On 6 June 1918 he found himself in the city of Tsaritsyn with a force of Red Guards and two armoured trains. Under the guise of 'director-general of food supplies' in south Russia, he began building his own empire, demanding soldiers and supplies from Moscow. In return he supplied food for the capital.

Stalin even became a kind of local warlord, launching military operations against the Whites. He achieved considerable successes and the city that held his headquarters was later named after him: Stalingrad. The conqueror returned a hero, to take his place beside Lenin. It was early days but Stalin could clearly see a route to power.

With other trusted aides travelling the country, Lenin found himself ever more dependent on Stalin, who became responsible for signing key orders. Stalin was something of a troubleshooter. All brash and brawn, he thought nothing of issuing the most ruthless diktats to advance Lenin's cause. As a right-hand man to the father of the revolution, Stalin was flexible and responsive and achieved results. He made it his business to know everybody who mattered – and everything they did. His nickname was 'Comrade Card-Index'.

Lenin increasingly relied on him, particularly so as the former's health began to fail. Lenin had never fully recovered from an attempt on his life made by a pistol-toting social democrat, Fanya Kaplan, in August 1918. Four years later he suffered a series of strokes, the last of which killed him on 21 January 1924.

By then, however, Lenin had completely fallen out with his old comrade. The final straw came shortly before his death when, in a telephone call, Stalin harshly insulted his wife Nadezhda Krupskaia. He called her 'a syphilitic whore' and, in her words, 'subjected me to a storm of the coarsest abuse'. Lenin's reaction is revealed in the words of his last testament: 'Stalin is too rude and this fault, quite tolerable in our midst or in relations among Communists, becomes intolerable for one who holds the office of General Secretary. Therefore I propose to the comrades that they consider a means of removing Stalin from the post and appointing to it another person … more patient, more loyal, more polite and more considerate to comrades, less capricious and so forth.'

After Lenin's death, Stalin was one of a trio who held the reigns of power on the Communist Party Central Committee. The other two were Leningrad party boss Grigory Zinoviev and his long-standing ally Lev Kamenev. But the greatest threat to Stalin's position came from Lenin's old defence chief Leon Trotsky, still closely

Demonstrations, initially peaceful, broke out across the nation in 1917. This newspaper image (above) is of a meeting in February in Erivan Square, Tiflis.

Popular uprisings from February 1917 onwards centred on the old Russian capital Petrograd (modern St Petersburg). In the city's Nevsky Prospekt troops opened fire on demonstrators.

The storming of Petrograd's Winter Palace as depicted in Sergei Eisenstein's film 'October: Ten Days that Shook the World'.

The cruiser *Aurora* shelled the Winter Palace, the seat of the Provisional Government, during the assault by Red Guards.

A Stalinist view of the October Revolution… Lenin and Stalin jointly plotting the downfall of the Provisional Government. In truth, Stalin's position in the Bolshevik leadership left him a spectator while Lenin and Trotsky organised the coup.

Отъ Военно-Революціоннаго Комитета при Петроградскомъ Совѣтѣ Рабочихъ и Солдатскихъ Депутатовъ.

Къ Гражданамъ Россіи.

Временное Правительство низложено. Государственная власть перешла въ руки органа Петроградскаго Совѣта Рабочихъ и Солдатскихъ Депутатовъ Военно-Революціоннаго Комитета, стоящаго во главѣ Петроградскаго пролетаріата и гарнизона.

Дѣло, за которое боролся народъ: немедленное предложеніе демократическаго мира, отмѣна помѣщичьей собственности на землю, рабочій контроль надъ производствомъ, созданіе Совѣтскаго Правительства — это дѣло обезпечено.

ДА ЗДРАВСТВУЕТЪ РЕВОЛЮЦІЯ РАБОЧИХЪ, СОЛДАТЪ И КРЕСТЬЯНЪ!

Военно-Революціонный Комитетъ при Петроградскомъ Совѣтѣ Рабочихъ и Солдатскихъ Депутатовъ.

25 октября 1917 г. 10 ч. утра.

The Decree of Soviet Power issued on 25 October 1917 (old style calendar) marked the foundation of the Soviet Union.

Stalin, shown here in Red Army uniform, had a civil war record of insubordination.

A well equipped Red Army company poses for the camera. The Bolshevik regime built its armed forces from a defeated and demoralised Tsarist army and untrained workers' militias.

In a painting glamourising his leadership, Stalin urges men of the 1st Cavalry Army into battle in 1919.

Vying for power… by the time this photograph was taken in 1919, Stalin believed he was of equal standing to Lenin, the revolutionary mastermind whom he had once hero-worshipped.

By 1922 obvious strains had appeared in the relationship between Stalin and Lenin but the latter's plans to curb the Georgian's power in the party was thwarted by his own poor health.

Lenin's wife Nadezhda Krupskaya had little love for Stalin whom she considered an ill-mannered bully.

Lenin, hero of the Revolution, pictured relaxing on holiday in early August 1922 after suffering the first of his debilitating strokes. He died in January 1924.

Leon Trotsky as a student and in later life. Along with Lenin, he was principal architect of the Russian Revolution but lost out to Stalin in the power struggle following Lenin's death. He was assassinated while in exile in Mexico in 1940.

identified with his former boss and a stalwart of Bolshevism. As war commissar between 1918 and 1920, he had proved himself through the creation of the Red Army and its ensuing successes. And he was far from impressed by Stalin, calling him 'the most outstanding mediocrity in our Party'.

Yet Trotsky's political position was weak. His radical philosophy of 'permanent revolution' required greater support than he could muster to allow him to bid for ultimate power. During the Revolution he had come into conflict with both Stalin and Zinoviev and their mutual antagonism had continued into the 1920s. So, for a while, Trotsky and Stalin skirted around one another like nervous pugilists, each with a different vision for the future. Stalin was for the moment satisfied to have control of the Soviet Union – or the Union of Soviet Socialist Republics (USSR) to give it its full title as established in 1922. Trotsky, by contrast, wanted to see revolution across the entire globe.

When battle was finally joined after Lenin's death, it was indeed over the future direction of the Soviet Union as a socialist state. Stalin took the unorthodox Marxist position that a proletariat revolution was possible in a comparatively backward country – Lenin's theory of the weakest link. Externally, he was concerned with fending off possible anti-Bolshevik interventions by capitalist countries. Internally, his aim was to drag ramshackle Russia into the modern age, no matter what the cost in terms of human misery. His policy was 'Socialism in one country'. Trotsky, on the other hand, believed the Soviet Union would founder unless revolutions occurred in the 'advanced capitalist' countries of Western Europe. The crux of his thinking was that working classes everywhere should accelerate the drive to overthrow the common enemy, capitalism.

The ground on which their battle was fought was economic policy. Trotsky and his followers supported the rapid industrialisation of the Soviet Union and the forced collectivisation of the peasants. At this time, Stalin sided with another leading Old Bolshevik, Nikolai Bukharin, in maintaining the so-called New Economic Policy, which favoured gradual industrialisation and paying independent smallholders a market price for their produce. In July 1926, following a long struggle over the direction of economic policy, Trotsky lost his seat in the Politburo. In November 1927 he was expelled from the party. In 1929 Stalin, knowing that the international revolutionary fanatic would remain a constant thorn in his side, banished Trotsky from the Soviet Union for ever.

It was not enough. From his places of exile, Trotsky waged a war of words against his old rival, accusing him of deviating from Leninist principles, and continued to contact potential anti-Stalin members of the party in the hope of forming an opposition bloc. He saw himself as an intellectual giant while Stalin was an ill-educated dwarf. Trotsky's writings attracted international attention. Author George

Bernard Shaw noted his vicious dexterity: 'When he cuts off his opponent's head, he holds it up to show that there are no brains in it.' Back in Moscow, Stalin was painfully aware that he could not match his enemy's skill with wit and words.

Eventually, the temperamental Soviet ruler could no longer tolerate his enemy's barbs. In 1936, following a show trial at which Trotsky was defendant in absentia, a warrant was issued for his arrest. Stalin handed the problem into the hands of his ruthless secret police, the NKVD (Russian acronym for People's Commissariat for International Affairs) and Trotsky's fate was sealed.

In 1937 Trotsky settled in Mexico and the country became a base for international revolutionary socialism. Enthusiastic couriers scuttled in and out to receive the wisdom of their great leader. His home was like a fortress, recently rebuilt after a bungled attempt on his life by the Mexican Communist Party, but one visitor who sought him out appeared innocuous enough to be granted an audience. Calling himself Frank Jacson, 'a Belgian mountaineer and writer', he arrived in Mexico in 1940 with his Canadian wife and asked Trotsky to help him with an article he was researching.

Trotsky welcomed him to his home on 20 August 1940, the guards readily opening the gates, unaware that under Jacson's coat was an alpine ice axe, a hammer and a .45 Estrella automatic. When the two men were alone in his study, Jacson pulled out the ice axe from his raincoat and smashed it down onto Trotsky's head. Trotsky lurched mortally wounded from the study to the drawing room, alerting the guards. Before lapsing into a coma, he told them to spare Jacson in order that he might talk.

Trotsky died 26 hours later in hospital. His assassin was really called Ramon Mercador, a Spanish-born committed Communist who had been hand-picked by the NKVD for the grisly killing and who was later hailed a hero in the Soviet Union.

*   *   *

From the time of Trotsky's fall from power in the mid-1920s, the authority of Josef Stalin was unrivalled – and he had big ambitions for the Soviet Union, longing to see his country at the top of the international industrial league. He wrote: 'We are fifty or a hundred years behind the advanced countries. We must make good this distance in ten years. Either we do it or we will be crushed.'

He was prepared to pay any price for the privilege of saving his nation – and that cost came in terms of human lives. For the path that Stalin followed in his quest led to the deaths of untold millions. People died of exhaustion, cold and starvation. In the name of Communism, Stalin exhibited the worst excesses of capitalism. As he did so, his people lived miserable existences in order to pursue the unattainable goals that his inhuman policies had set them.

Grand plans for industrial centres were drawn up. The first so-called Five Year Plan was carried out between 1928 and 1932 with some success. People worked hard with a will to please the leadership. One Ukrainian miner, Alexei Stakhanov, cut out 102 tons of coal in one shift instead of the usual seven. He was heralded as a hero of the revolution.

It was impossible to maintain this level of production across the board for long, and the rewards presented to workers were few. Conditions were grim, strikes banned and, in a climate of industrial repression, workers flitted from job to job. A worker in the coal and iron ore industries in 1930 stayed in a job for an average of just four months. When targets were not met, Stalin declared that there were wreckers or saboteurs at work and show trials were held to root them out.

Nevertheless, the lure of employment in industry still drew thousands of peasants from the country to the town. Accordingly, there were fewer people producing food, and those who were producing grain were belligerent because the price offered by the government was so meagre. By 1928 the production of food was so low that the towns, with their freshly boosted populations, began to starve. So did the men of the Red Army. Stalin knew that danger loomed if discontent spread within the ranks of the powerful armed forces and countered this with portents of doom.

In speeches, Stalin made mention of the threat of war and the need to strengthen the Soviet state for the coming conflict. Looking back, there was scant evidence for this view, which was little more than illusion wrought by Stalin to rally the people. Yet it worked, for a brutal era got under way with barely an organised protest from the masses.

One measure Stalin could have taken was to have raised the price of grain, which would have stimulated its supply and better fed the people. But it would have immediately made it more expensive for those living in cities and towns who, according to Marxist theory, were the backbone of the proletarian state. And Stalin, the son of a serf, now felt himself too elevated to be at the mercy of the peasants. Suspicions that they were withholding grain as part of an organised opposition to socialism festered in his mind. His answer was to collectivise agriculture. Collectivisation meant state ownership of the land and its crops. Hand in hand came mechanisation of agriculture.

To inspire support for this radical measure, he focussed the blame for his country's hard times on the Kulaks, peasants who owned land and were small-scale food producers. In Tsarist Russia, the Kulak was a peasant with a reasonable amount of land who needed to hire farmhands at harvest time and was generally perceived as a rapacious profiteer. The October Revolution had supposedly done away with this class of farmer but there were still many who, by dint of luck or hard work, had become comparatively prosperous during the 1920s. They were least likely to favour collectivisation and could easily be demonised as small-scale exploiters of the poorer peasants.

Stalin at his desk. In 1929 he wrote for the newspaper Pravda: 'We are advancing full steam ahead to socialism, leaving behind the age-old Russian backwardness.'

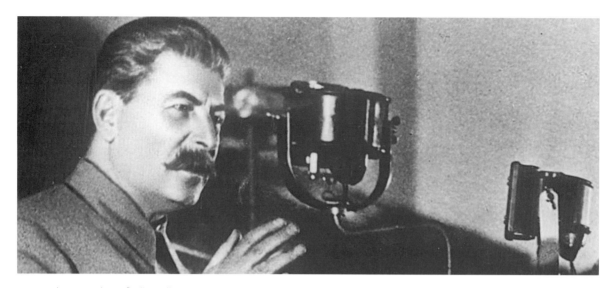

In speeches, Stalin railed against the classes in society he blamed for obstructing his promised Communist Utopia. Foremost were the kulaks, peasant smallholders whom he demonised and whose land he turned over to 'collectivised' farming.

A stage-managed demonstration on a collective farm in 1930. The banner reads: 'Liquidate the kulaks as a class.'

Members of the Komsomol (Communist Youth League) unearthing bags of grain hidden by kulak peasants in a cemetery near Odessa.

The Soviet Gulag was a vast system of forced labour camps, through which 20 million people are estimated to have passed – among which these chained 'slaves' were a handful.

Back-breaking construction work at Gulags in Siberia.

Paintings like this were commissioned to encourage the cult of personality that was to dominate Soviet culture. Here the artist commemorates Stalin's visit to a hydro-electric project in the Caucasus in 1931.

The supposed success of 'collectivisation' is demonstrated by this unlikely scene of Ukrainian farm workers enjoying the bounty of their toil.

Stalin inspects a new model of caterpillar tractor in 1935. Standing at his side is party henchman Sergo Ordzhonikidze, who committed suicide two years later at the height of Stalin's political show trials.

Stalin used the Soviet propaganda machine to identify himself with 'heroic' workers such as these cotton growers.

The first Five Year Plan (1928-1933) saw a mass movement of people from the countryside to industrial areas. These workers from Belorussia are on their way east to the vast experimental developments of the Kuzbass 'Autonomous Industrial Colony' in Western Siberia.

These Kulaks were to suffer endless misery and degradation. Their smallholdings were swallowed up by the state and five million of them were deported as forced labour to the bleak northern regions of the country, where they died in droves. Along with them went many others who were not Kulaks but who opposed Stalin or had found the courage to speak out against collectivisation. One observer at the time noted: 'The best and hardest workers of the land are being taken away, with the misfits and the lazybones staying behind.'

Stalin was rightly concerned about the backward state of agriculture, with peasants reliant on horse and harrow rather than on machinery to ease their burden and improve output. But his methods of enforcement were barbaric and he showed little remorse for the havoc that he was wreaking. As he justified his policy, he branded Kulaks 'the sworn enemies of collectivisation'. He announced: 'Our policy is a class policy. He who thinks that one can conduct in the countryside a policy which will please everyone, the rich as well as the poor, is not a Marxist but an idiot because, comrades, such a policy does not exist in the natural order of things.'

Indeed, Stalin vowed to 'cleanse' the country of Kulaks — and the language he used paralleled the denunciation of the Jews by Hitler during his despotic regime. Stalin announced: 'To take the offensive against the Kulaks means to deal the Kulak class such a blow that it will never again rise to its feet. Of course the Kulak can't be admitted to a collective farm. He can't because he is an accursed enemy.'

The remaining peasants were often far from keen on the prospect of joining a collective. Before their hour came, they slaughtered their stock and gorged themselves, fearful that they were losing everything and would be getting nothing at all on a shared Communist-style farm. In 1930 almost a quarter of Russia's peasants were forced into collectives. Six years later 90 per cent of the peasant population had been 'collectivised'. The complexion of the entire countryside was changed beyond recognition and at unprecedented speed. Stalin refused to pace the changes. 'To slow down the tempo would mean falling behind,' he said,' and those who fall behind get beaten.'

The famine that loomed in the towns and cities during 1928 returned to haunt the countryside in the early 'Thirties. Rural chaos reigned, with little being sown and all the produce being dispatched away as soon as it was ready. Stories abounded of mothers killing and eating their children, of a trade in human flesh for food. The hungry and the desperate ground bones and leather to make flour and scavenged in the undergrowth for insects and small mammals. Perhaps the full horrors will never be known.

Lev Kopelev was one of the eager young Communists who requisitioned food from distraught peasants and their hungry families. His fanatical ideology is evidenced by the following chilling statement: 'Our great goal was the universal triumph of Communism, and for the sake of that goal, everything was permissible – to lie, to steal, to destroy hundreds of thousands and even millions of people.'

As food was shipped out of the countryside to the towns, the hungry peasants were tempted to hoard or to sabotage the transport that was taking away their salvation. In response, Stalin ordered trials, with children accusing their parents of crimes against the state. By 1932 Stalin had forbidden collective farmers from leaving their villages.

Collectivisation had produced some statistical success. State purchase of grain doubled between 1928 and 1931 while exports soared. For Stalin was content to send the majority of food produced in the USSR abroad as a means of trumpeting his successes and in order to find the money to pay for an ambitious factory building programme – even though the bodies of the starving littered the streets. That peak soon passed. By 1935, production had slumped. The lesson that an unhappy workforce did not work well appeared lost on Stalin, who later admitted that as many as ten million had perished. Yet his attitude towards death was bizarre. 'One death is a tragedy,' he would say, 'a million just statistics'.

*   *   *

There were two deaths among the millions that did affect Stalin, however… the loss of his wives, one from typhoid, the other by suicide. The death of the first rendered him distraught. The death of the second simply enraged him.

When Joseph Stalin married for the first time, the bride was chosen by his mother. Teacher's daughter Yekaterina Svanidze, nicknamed 'Kato', was Stalin's social superior and seemingly uninterested in politics yet she agreed to wed the brash, uncouth revolutionary socialist. Some reports have him marrying her while in prison in 1903 – not an unusual occurrence in those days – but it is more likely that he put aside his atheism to marry her in an Orthodox church in the Georgian capital Tiflis in 1906.

Little is know of their life together, which was to be cut tragically short. Two months after giving birth to their son Yakov in March 1907, Kato died of typhoid fever. As he stood by her coffin, Stalin told a friend: 'This creature softened my stony heart. When she died all warm feeling for people died with her. It is all so desolate here inside, so inexpressibly empty.'

His son Yakov was ignored by Stalin and instead was brought up by Kato's brother, Alexander, an old friend and mutual revolutionary. Stalin was to repay his dedication by having him, his wife and sister thrown into prison on trumped-up treason charges in 1937. They were executed in February 1941. That same year, Yako, by then a Red Army soldier, was captured by the Germans and sent to Sachsenhausen concentration camp. There he is believed to have been shot by a guard or to have thrown himself onto an electric fence – his father having previously rejected an offer to free him in a senior prisoner exchange.

Meanwhile, twelve years after the death of his first wife, Stalin had remarried. His chosen bride was 17-year-old Nadezhda Sergeevna, daughter of his revolutionary comrade Sergei Alliluyev – whose wife he had already slept with. It is rumoured that he began his relationship with the teenager, nicknamed Nadya, by raping her during a train journey. Only when her father discovered the attack did 39-year-old Stalin propose marriage.

Soon after they wed, Nadya bore him a son, Vasily. Five years later they had a daughter, Svetlana. Yakov, Stalin's son by his first marriage, also joined the household — as did the infant Artyom Sergeev, whom Stalin formally adopted after his father, a revolutionary hero, was killed in 1921. For a brief period of normality, home life might even have suited Stalin the family man. He enjoyed his children's company, particularly Svetlana's whom he called 'my Little Sparrow'. He even put aside his state papers to help with her homework. He was an avid reader, eventually boasting a library of 40,000 books. His other passion was for film, ironically favouring Hollywood movies including Westerns and Charlie Chaplin comedies. In the evening he would play billiards or light a pipe and listen to Georgian folk music while downing fine Georgian wine. With cronies, he would continue drinking late into the night, which accounted for his nocturnal preference, not retiring until the early hours and often not rising before noon. Despite his alcoholic excesses, he was said to be courteous to his servants – though not always to his spouse.

Nadya, however, had difficulty in adapting to life as a wife and mother. Her family were all revolutionaries and women were treated as equals to men but Stalin felt differently. The role he had in mind for his wife was a submissive one. Nadya could not and would not conform. To escape the closeted drudgery of life in the Kremlin, Nadya became an aide to Lenin. He confided in her implicitly and entrusted her with the most secret documents. In return, her loyalty to him and the party far outweighed her burden of duty to her husband. Stalin was regularly outraged when she refused to share these secrets with her. After Lenin's death, Nadya went to work for a magazine titled Revolution And Culture, once again revelling in her independence.

At home, the children were brought up by nannies. The household was run by a housekeeper, a cook and the guards of the secret police. She and her husband slept in separate rooms, she in a finely appointed bedroom with plush rugs and Chanel scent bottles dotting the dressing table, he in a study next to his governmental red telephone.

There were bitter rows between the pair. She had run away from him once in 1926 hoping to start a new life but he had summoned her back. She became prone to depression, for days sinking into unreachable black moods. During the frequent blazing rows she had with Stalin, usually after his heavy drinking, he would accuse her of being schizophrenic. She would call him paranoid.

By way of escape, Nadya threw herself into work. She studied at the Industrial Academy and aimed to become an engineer. But Stalin still overshadowed her existence as fellow students were persecuted and sent to the harsh prison labour camps of the Siberian Gulag. Old comrades, people she had known and trusted all her life, were being branded enemies of the state. A passionate socialist, her unease about the conditions of the peasants and workers was growing. Her discomfort at the direction of the regime with her husband at the helm grew ever greater, yet she was powerless to intervene. Nadya sought solace in religion, one of the few overt ways that she exploited her position as wife to Stalin. While worship was banned by the regime and churches desecrated, Nadya was permitted to pursue her religious beliefs in relative peace.

If she struggled to come to terms with her unhappy life, still worse was to come. During one of their terrible arguments Stalin revealed a shocking truth. He had been sleeping with her mother around the time Nadya was conceived. She confronted her mother, who admitted that she had been bedding Stalin at the time, along with her husband and perhaps one other. The bombshell nearly broke her – for it was theoretically possible that Stalin could have been both her husband and father.

By the time of the fifteenth anniversary of the October Revolution in 1932, the pressure on Nadya was intense. Officials at the celebration parade remarked on her aged face, its grey-white colour and lifeless eyes. That night there was a party for the upper echelons of the Kremlin. Stalin was as coarse and bullying as ever. In his drunkenness he noticed his wife's empty glass and was irritated by it. 'Oi you, drink,' he bellowed.

'Don't talk to me like that,' screamed Nadya. She stormed out of the party, pursued by Paulina Molotov, wife of Vyacheslav, a high ranking Bolshevik. Paulina did her best to soothe Nadya and parted only when she appeared calm once more. She was the last person to see her alive. The next morning a housekeeper found Nadya's cold body lying in a pool of blood, a small pistol by her side. Stalin was asleep nearby, recovering from his stupor of the night before. Instead of waking him, the housekeeper called Paulina Molotov and another old friend of Nadya's family. It was their grief-stricken wails that finally awoke the dictator.

Her death, according to the newspapers, was due to appendicitis. Her daughter Svetlana who was six at the time, was never told the gory truth and only discovered it by chance when reading a magazine in London at the age of 15. Rumour flew around Moscow, however. Stalin was said to have murdered his wife after discovering an affair between her and his son Yakov. Suicide was impossible, declared the gossips, the fatal bullet having penetrated her left temple when she was right-handed.

Stalin's first wife Yekaterina Svanidze, nicknamed 'Kato'.

Stalin (right) stands over the coffin of Kato after her death of typhoid shortly after giving birth to their son in 1907. Her distraught husband said: 'When she died all warm feeling for people died with her.'

A picture believed to be of Stalin with his second wife Nadezhda Sergeevna, whom he had met when she was just 17. It is rumoured that they were forced to wed after he raped her on a train.

Nadya, as she was known, with daughter Svetlana. She was, by all accounts, a strict and puritanical influence on her family. She was also tough. When she gave birth to their first child, Vasily, in 1921 she walked to hospital.

Nadya lying in state after her mysterious death which, according to newspapers, was due to appendicitis. In fact, she was found lying in a pool of blood with a pistol at her side.

Nadya's elaborate funeral cortege. Stalin, who walked behind the coffin, never recovered from her suicide.

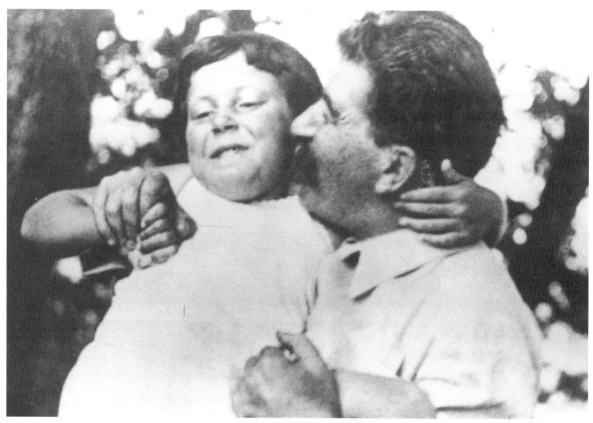

Stalin showed particular affection for his daughter Svetlana, pictured here with him in the early 1930s.

Stalin with Svetlana and Vasily, whom his father described as a 'spoilt boy of average abilities'.

Svetlana had a privileged childhood, although her relationship with her father faded in her teenage years. She was never told the gory truth about her mother's death and only discovered it by chance at the age of 15.

Reports on the death were subsequently destroyed so it is impossible to verify the cause today but, given her state of mind, it is likely that Nadya did indeed take her own life. Her family maintained there was a suicide note in which she railed against Stalin personally and his policies generally.

Stalin was almost certainly scarred by the incident. He was not only bereft but furious too. He vowed to shun her burial but later relented. 'She crippled me,' he said mournfully, adding more acidly: 'She went away as an enemy.'

Of the children of this unhappy union and of his previous relationships, little was revealed to Stalin's subjects over the years. But their fates were variously remarkable...

We have seen how his first son Yakov was abandoned by his father and died as a prisoner of war in a German concentration camp. His second child was similarly hidden from sight. He was Konstantin Kuzakov, the illegitimate son Stalin fathered by his landlady in 1911 while living in exile in the isolated village Solvychegodsk. Stalin's exile ended and he departed while his lover Maria was still pregnant. The boy never had any contact with his father, later sighting him only once at close quarters but too nervous to address him. In 1932 he was forced by the NKVD to sign an agreement never to reveal his parentage and did not do so until after Stalin's death. Following service as a colonel in World War II, Konstantin Kuzakov was arrested in 1947 accused of being a US spy but was freed, probably on Stalin's orders, and returned to his career as an academic in Leningrad. He died in 1996.

Stalin's children by his second wife Nadya went in very different directions. Vasily was brought up by nannies after his mother's apparent suicide. His father described him as a 'spoilt boy of average abilities', which seems to have been an accurate appraisal. Vasily abused his family status both socially and professionally, becoming a playboy, a drunkard and a womaniser, despite being twice married. He trained as a pilot but was notorious for commandeering planes and flying them while inebriated.

Promoted to general at the start of World War II, a rank far above his abilities, he was deeply unpopular because of his intolerable temper. His father once ordered him dismissed from the air service for 'hard drinking, debauchery and corrupting the regiment' but later had him reinstated. After Stalin's death, Vasily was arrested for 'misappropriation of state property' and served seven years before being released in 1960. He was arrested a year later for causing a traffic accident and was exiled to the Tartar city of Kazan where, his health ruined, he died aged 40 in 1962.

Stalin's only daughter, Svetlana, was more successful, becoming a lecturer, writer and a sought-after literary translator, fluent in English, German and French. She had mixed success with her relationships, however, as a 16-year-old falling in love with a 40-year-old Soviet filmmaker who happened to be Jewish. Stalin got him out of the way by having him sentenced to ten years in exile close to the Arctic Circle.

Vasily Stalin was over-privileged and over-promoted. A habitual drunkard, he used his father's name to further his career, to obtain government perks and to seduce a string of women.

Svetlana went on to marry three times and had three children. In 1963 she fell in love with an Indian Communist but they were not allowed to marry. When in 1966 he died of emphysema, she was permitted to take his ashes back to India – and from there caused an international furore by defecting to the USA, where she became naturalised and briefly married an American citizen. In the 1980s she flitted between the US, England and Russia where she was regranted citizenship in 1984. Svetlana died of cancer in Wisconsin aged 85 in 2011.

* * *

If, throughout his adult life, Stalin had showed scant regard for his family, his indifference was nothing compared to his treatment of former political bedfellows and millions of suffering innocents in the grim decade before the Second World War.

By 1934 Stalin held sway over the Soviet Union as General Secretary and, although his power was not absolute, he had ensured that key jobs were held by his supporters. However, there was a politburo that could overrule him and candidates sufficiently popular to take his place. Stalin decided to make his position unassailable with one of the bloodiest episodes of modern times, the Great Purge.

It was sparked by the murder of Sergei Kirov, a party bigwig in Leningrad. His assassin was a disgruntled Communist called Leonid Nikolayev who lurked in the toilets of the Smolny Institute in Leningrad before leaping out and shooting him in the back of the neck.

While Kirov had once been a close associate of Stalin, the gulf between the two had been growing. Kirov had been championing the cause of the workers and had demanded that Stalin improve conditions both in industry and agriculture. Kirov was also being proposed as an alternative General Secretary by those in the party left unconvinced by Stalin's brand of Communism.

Opposition to Stalin emerged in 1932 in the form of an authoritative document, the so-called 'Ryutin Platform', that indicted him with a betrayal of Leninism. Largely written by senior party functionary Martemyan Ryutin, it called for rebellion among the peasants, the removal of Stalin and the release of Trotskyites from prison. Stalin wanted Comrade Ryutin and his cohorts shot but the politburo refused to allow it. Instead he was imprisoned and the so-called Ryutin Counter-revolutionary Group were expelled from the party. They included Grigory Zinoviev and Lev Kamenev, both respected Old Bolsheviks who had once shared power with Stalin but had been the target of his venom for years.

The shooting of Sergei Kirov had given Stalin a lever to use against his still-active opponents. He may even have organised it himself. The instant consequence was that scores of people were accused of complicity in the crime, anyone who appeared in the files of the secret police being arrested and interrogated. The charges were then expanded to cover those considered enemies of the Soviet Union. Thousands were deported to Gulag labour camps in Siberia where they perished.

Then the show trials began. The first got underway in 1935 and it was repeated the following year. In the dock on both occasions were Zinoviev and Kamenev. Evidence against the defendants was virtually non-existent, with confessions clearly having been wrung out of them, but that did not stop Prosecutor-General Andrei Vyshinsky branding them 'mad dogs of capitalism'. The two were sentenced to death and executed almost immediately. Such was the thrall of Stalin that they went to their deaths urging the Russian people to follow their leader.

In the following two years there was a frenzy of death, denunciation and paranoia among the population. Gulag camps were bursting at the seams, with an estimated population of eight million. Mass graves were needed to cope with the number of bodies.

A succession of public trials seemed to reveal that virtually the whole of the old Bolshevik leadership had at some time or another plotted the downfall of the Soviet Union and the assassination of Comrade Stalin. In January 1937 a group associated with Trotsky were tried and most found guilty. One, Georgi Piatakov, was a close associate of Stalin supporter Sergo Ordzhonikidze, who committed suicide shortly after Piatakov's guilt was established. In June 1937 a secret trial wiped out a substantial part of the Red Army's high command, including its best military brain, Marshal Mikhail Tukhachevsky, who happened to have been a friend of Kirov.

The last great show trial of this period was held in March 1938 when 21 so-called 'right deviationists', including Stalin's former friend Nikolai Bukharin and his ally Alexsei Rykov, were found guilty of treason and executed. The only old Bolsheviks now left were all Stalinists.

By now the Soviet Union had entered the so-called 'Ezhovschina' (Ezhov's Time) named after the fanatical NKVD chief Nikolai Ezhov, when the purges were at their height and hundreds of thousands perished. The string of show trials had been initiated under his predecessor, ex-policeman Genrikh Yagoda, whom Stalin dismissed in 1936 and executed two years later. But under Ezhof, the NKVD pursued their task with extra relish.

Possessing unseemly enthusiasm, they burst into the homes of sleeping families and hauled off innocent victims for torture, beatings, exile or execution. There is evidence that the NKVD worked on a quota system, killing to fulfil a body count.

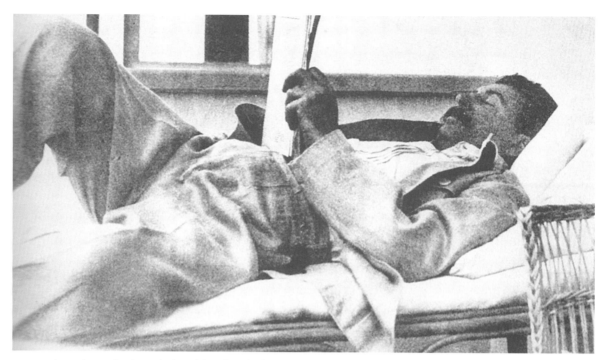

At a time of ruinous industrial and agricultural policies and of vicious political purges, Stalin relaxes at his country dacha.

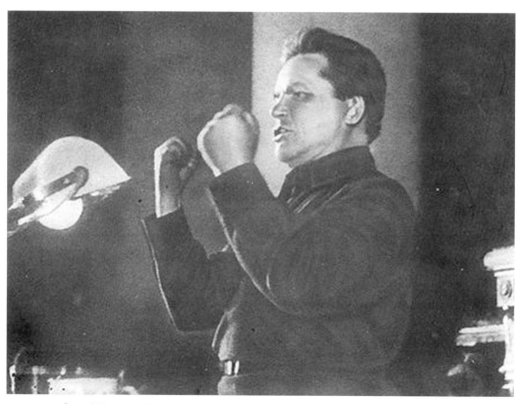

Sergei Kirov, the Communist Party chief in Leningrad, was assassinated in December 1934. Although Stalin may have organised the killing, he nevertheless used it as an excuse to lock up scores of supposed 'conspirators'.

When celebrated author Maksim Gorki died in 1936 Stalin helped bear his coffin – although it was later suggested that he had actually ordered his poisoning.

Posters of party leaders cover the wooden buildings in Svirlag labour camp, near Leningrad, in 1936.

Now you see him, now you don't… At about 5ft 5ins (1.65m), Stalin was sensitive about his height, which was why it is likely that a diminutive soldier was added to this doctored photograph!

After Nikolai Ezhov succeeded Genrikh Yagoda as head of the NKVD in 1936, state terror reached new heights. Ezhov disappeared from public view in 1939 and was secretly shot in 1940.

Ezhov was followed as secret service boss by the equally ruthless Lavrenti Beria. He suffered the same fate as his predecessor, being shot in 1953 just a few months after Stalin's death.

Steely-eyed as ever, the Soviet 'Man of Steel' poses for this official photograph.

Anyone and everyone was suspected of 'counter-revolutionary' activity. Minds twisted by Stalinism applied this to all manner of incidents. A faithful belief in Stalin and devotion to the motherland was not sufficient to prevent death. Trials were few and those held were rarely just. The purge spread its tentacles into all walks of life, including the army, navy, Old Bolsheviks, academics, historians, railway workers, engineers, statisticians and teachers. Finally, the NKVD reaped its grim reward and was itself purged in 1939. Ezhov was replaced by Lavrentiy Beria, a Georgian who took a personal interest in the art of torture and was referred to by Stalin as 'my Himmler', a reference to Hitler's evil SS chief.

Now no one would dare challenge Stalin's authority. Even a whisper of insurrection was as good as the death penalty. Yet his country was sterile, with the cream of its talent laid waste in nameless graves. A final body count will never be known. But worse was to come...

* * *

Before the outbreak of the Second World War, Britain and France had been courting Stalin. As war with Nazi Germany loomed, both governments saw the need to forget past differences and enlist the support of the Soviet tyrant. Hitler had other ideas; the Führer had made no secret of his loathing of Communism as an ideal and the Russian people as sub-human Slavs. Yet in August 1939 Hitler performed a staggering diplomatic U-turn. Out of the blue came the Berlin-Moscow Non-Aggression Pact, signed at the Kremlin by Foreign Ministers Joachim von Ribbentrop for Germany and Vyacheslav Mikhailovich Molotov for the Soviet Union.

On the face of it, there were admirable, mutual benefits. Germany would receive grain and oil in exchange for technology. Each promised not to attack the other. However, the real reason for the agreement, a secret protocol that went unpublished until Germany's surrender in 1945, was masked by those pledges of cordiality. Within two weeks, Hitler and his troops had marched into Poland. The Poles were soon crushed in a lightning war and their country was carved up, with Germany occupying the west and the Red Army moving into the east.

The subjugation of Poland was the most tangible 'benefit' of the pact that Stalin had sought. It gave him a taste for expansion. He looked towards neighbouring Finland. In November 1939 he demanded territory from the tiny country. When its government refused to relinquish the land, the Red Army marched in. But if Stalin was hoping for a German-style quick victory, he was sorely disappointed. Finland was the 'mouse that roared'. Within six weeks, the country's gallant guerrilla fighters had wreaked havoc with the enemy forces. It was not until March 1940 that Finland was finally brought to heel — by which time more than 150,000 Red Army soldiers had lost their lives. This small country had humiliated its giant neighbour, much to Stalin's chagrin.

There was no one to blame for the poor performance of the army other than Stalin himself. The purge had relieved the Red Army of its finest leaders. By the end of 1938, three out of every five marshals were dead, as well as 13 out of 15 army commanders. More than half of the country's divisional commanders had lost their lives. The Red Army, the largest in the world, suffered from an acute shortage of direction and know-how. Those left to assume command were generally the worst and weakest.

Hitler watched with interest the failings of the Red Army in action. The ill-conceived war against Finland confirmed his belief that the 'Russian bear' could be beaten. The Führer's hidden agenda – of war against Stalin, the Soviet Union and its people – came to the fore.

The spring of 1941 brought a distraction for Hitler in the Balkans when his forces attacked Greece and Yugoslavia. Victory was quick and Hitler turned his attention back to Russia. It was a late spring, and Russia's primitive roads were left clogged by mud during the slow thaw, so it was not until June that an attack against Russia was deemed appropriate.

On the morning of 22 June 1941, as the last trainload of grain under the Hitler-Stalin Pact chugged westward out of the Soviet Union by train, German soldiers poured in. 'Operation Barbarossa', Hitler's masterplan for German expansion in the east, had begun.

As events transpired, Hitler's attack on Russia at that time may well have been the greatest misjudgment of the Second World War. If so, the second greatest mistake was Stalin's reaction to it. Or, rather, his lack of reaction. At the end of the conflict, when the analyses of the conduct of the war were made and the reckoning taken, it was Stalin's personal handling of his greatest crisis that was the most discreditable. History was not favourable to the Georgian bully who hid at the first sign of trouble…

In spring 1941, as German forces mustered on the Soviet Union's southerly borders, dire warnings had been dispatched to Stalin of the impending attack. Historians have noted that as many as 76 different alerts were sent to Moscow. Britain's Prime Minister Winston Churchill was happy to bury the differences of the past in order to prepare Stalin. Spies from across the world sent back the alarming news. One German soldier, a committed Communist, even deserted to bring word of Hitler's intentions to Stalin well in time for his forces to react.

However, nothing could persuade stubborn Stalin that his ally Germany would break its pact. If an attack was going to come, he felt certain it would be from Japan. Such was his faith in Hitler that he ordered his commanders not to fortify the border. Stalin even had the runaway German soldier shot.

Stalin was lucky to have a military genius heading his armies. He was the Chief of

Staff, General Georgy Zhukov, who on the afternoon of 21 June – the eve of war – was sufficiently confident in his border intelligence units to hand his leader a piece of paper bearing the draft of a directive to the Soviet armed forces placing them on maximum alert. Stalin handed it back, saying gruffly: 'This order is premature. Draw up another to the effect that on the night of 21-22 June there may be provocation on the border. The troops must be ready for it but they must not be incited by any provocations which might lead to complications.'

Zhukov scurried away to redraft the warning. The final, approved version was not in fact issued until the early hours of Sunday 22 June and were not read by many front-line commanders until they were actually under shellfire! Only one element of the armed forces, the Navy, had by that time been mobilised for war – and then only on its own initiative. In the end, it was the navy that first alerted the Kremlin to the fact that the country was being invaded.

At 3.15am the commander of the Black Sea Fleet telephoned the Kremlin with the news that the Luftwaffe was bombing the Sebastopol naval base. The call was taken by Admiral Nikolai Kuznetsov, the duty naval commissar at the Kremlin, who, prepared for the crisis, had set up a camp bed in his office. The admiral immediately tried to contact Stalin's office. When Admiral Kuznetsov finally got through, the duty officer told him: 'He's not here and I don't know where he is.' In fact, the Soviet leader had been driven to his villa outside the city and had gone to bed leaving orders not to be disturbed.

Around 4.30am, the very moment that the entire might of the Nazi military machine was being thrown against the unprepared Russian armies across the entire front, Zhukov himself finally telephoned Stalin's villa. The phone rang and rang until eventually the sleepy voice of an officer answered. In response to the Chief of Staff's urgent summons, the man could only blurt out: 'Comrade Stalin is asleep.' Zhukov commanded: 'Wake him up immediately. The Germans are bombing our cities.'

It was several minutes more before Stalin picked up the phone. When Zhukov outlined the scale of the catastrophe, Stalin fell silent. 'Do you understand me?' Zhukov pleaded. His leader answered by calling a meeting of the Politburo.

By the time the political leadership had been hastily assembled, the spring sunshine was filtering through the trees of the Moscow parks. Stalin stunned his audience by asking: 'Don't you think all this might be a provocation?' Even at 7.15pm, with his border defences blasted apart in a hundred places, Stalin was still clinging to the hope that this was not a 'real attack' and seeking 'clarification of the position' from his envoys in Berlin. He ordered that the Red Army repel the invaders but not retaliate by entering German occupied territory.

Hours later, he realised that he had been duped by a greater dictator. Staring into space, devoid of emotion as well as action, he said simply: 'All that Lenin created we have lost forever.' Then he ordered his car and retreated to his villa – not to be seen for ten days.

Sunday 22 June 1941 was a fine day in Moscow. Families promenaded in the warmth. At 11.30am the loudspeakers in the main streets, which traditionally played marches and light music, a voice suddenly broke in: 'Vnimaniye! Vnimaniye!' (Attention! Attention!)

The Muscovites listened in anticipation as an announcer told them that there was to be important broadcast at noon. The music did not return. Instead a metronome began ticking. At noon, as promised, the metronome stopped. Then the Foreign Minister, Vyacheslav Molotov, spoke:

'Men and women, citizens of the Soviet Union, the Soviet government and its head, Comrade Stalin, have instructed me to make the following announcement. At 4am, without declaration of war and without any claims being made on the Soviet Union, German troops attacked our country, attacked our frontier in many places and bombed from the air Zhitomir, Kiev, Sebastopol, Kaunus and other cities. The attack has been made despite the fact that there was a non-aggression pact between the Soviet Union and Germany, a pact the terms of which were scrupulously observed by the Soviet Union. Our cause is just. The enemy will be crushed. Victory will be ours.'

There was a moment's stunned silence, then pandemonium. Over the next few hours, fearful Muscovites tried to draw their money out of the banks and headed for the jewellery shops, where most of the cash was exchanged for safer forms of investment. They also swept through the city's food stores, stocking up for the siege of their country that they knew was coming.

If they ever wondered why Molotov had made the dramatic announcement rather than Stalin, they probably assumed that their leader was busying himself with the war effort. They could not have been wrong. Joseph Stalin sat in his villa in a state of near paralysis. As war had loomed, he had failed miserably in his judgment. With war begun, he failed miserably in his leadership.

'Operation Barbarossa', Germany's codename for the attack on the Soviet Union, involved 2,500,000 men in 165 divisions. The assault came in three prongs, one headed for Kiev, the next for Leningrad and a third for Moscow. Russian commanders were flummoxed because of Stalin's inertia as the Red Army fell back in disarray. The Soviet leader was only stung into action when it became clear that many of his people were not resisting the Nazis but welcoming them as liberators.

In communities along the front, long-silent church bells rang out – not to warn against but to welcome the invaders. In the newly occupied towns, Christians, for years refused the right to worship, joyfully assembled in churches for services. In addition, many civilians, especially peasant farmers, welcomed what seemed to be an end to the purges and the beginnings of the freedoms promised in 1917. Even the Jews, victims of Stalin's anti-semitism, responded willingly to Nazi posters asking them to register with the invaders.

As Hitler predicted, the Red Army was no match for the skill of his Wehrmacht. Stalin, who had little military experience or intuition, at first disappeared from public view but after 3 July 1941 he exerted total control over Soviet strategy. His initial reply to the German onslaught was to order his men to stand firm, then to launch ill-advised, ill-organised counterattacks. Those who retreated were considered cowards and shot. However, the situation as the Red Army recoiled from the frontiers was so confused that it is unlikely that Stalin could have altered events even if he had been history's greatest military genius. The prospects for the Russian soldiers were grim.

Disillusioned troops, assured by their leaders that invasion was impossible, surrendered by the tens of thousand. In less than six months, the conquering army of just over three million were to capture almost two-an-a-half million of the Red Army. In German hands, the prisoners were treated with contempt, deprived of food, clothes and adequate shelter. Thousands were sent back to Germany to almost certain death in the Nazi labour camps.

Hitler was dazzled by the success of his conquering forces. 'Russia will be finished in three weeks', his generals told him. The only blot on his horizon was the way the motorised Panzer divisions had outpaced the infantry. Within two months of hectic advances, Hitler decided it was time for a breathing space. He ordered front-line generals to veer away from their principal target Moscow to Kiev. The generals were astonished and horrified. Even after Kiev had fallen, Moscow and Leningrad remained still some distance away from the leading German units. Hitler's generals were rightly concerned about the risks of being entrenched outside the cities during the harsh Russian winter. Before long the first autumn rains came, to be followed by the first chill of winter. Residents of both cities made good use of the unexpected respite. As the Germans fumed in abeyance, the Russians fortified their cities with anti-tank ditches, barbed-wire walls and earthworks.

The resumed German advance was handicapped by boggy roads, broken machinery and weary men and horses. At the gates of Moscow the German army was brought to a standstill. Happily, although the enemy was in the western suburbs, Muscovites were still receiving supplies from the east. In Leningrad there was a siege that held fast for 900 days. In the encircled city two million citizens died from starvation, privation and disease before the cordon was lifted.

Above and opposite top: Twin tyrants… It still remains a mystery as to how two such ogres as Hitler and Stalin could have dominated huge nations, territories and 20th-century history.

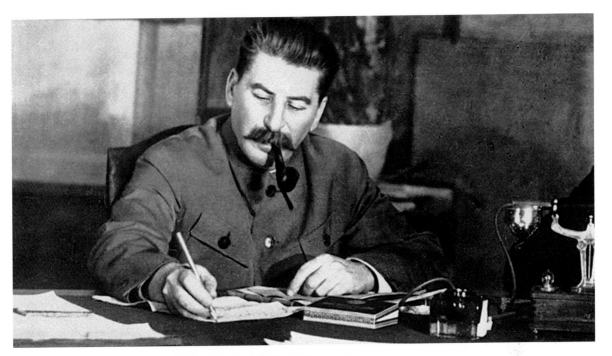

A propaganda poster urges Soviet citizens to defend the Motherland against the Nazis.

Muscovite men queue to receive their mobilisation orders after the German invasion on 22 June 1941.

Red Army soldiers on their way to the front march through Leningrad under the eyes of a statue of Kirov.

Women and elderly men dig anti-tank trenches during the autumn of 1941.

The rains and mud on the Eastern Front in both spring and autumn were a serious hindrance to both sides.

A Red Army nurse struggles to help a wounded comrade to safety.

Stalin's first-born, Yakov, captured by the Germans in 1941. Offered his freedom in a prisoner exchange, Stalin refused and Yakov died in a concentration camp.

The war initially went badly for Stalin. Here the Axis leaders Hitler and Mussolini inspect captured territory on the Russian Front.

A T34 tank is repaired in a tractor factory during the defence of Stalingrad.

An air raid during Leningrad's 872-day siege.

Russian tanks roll through the streets of Leningrad.

Bodies lie in the street after a bombardment of Leningrad in 1942.

All smiles…
Stalin welcomes
Winston
Churchill to the
Kremlin in
August 1942.

Georgy Zhukov, Russia's most successful commander of World War Two.

German prisoners captured in Stalingrad are marched away to camps in February 1943.

The winter weather came to the rescue of Russia, just as it had in 1812 when Napoleon's forces were defeated. German soldiers dug in to experience the miseries of freezing months spent in the open. Hundreds were killed by enemy action during the winter deadlock but many thousands more fell victim to frostbite.

Also to Russia's advantage were the enormous volumes of manpower summoned to fight for the motherland. The Soviet Union encompassed many races and nationalities. So while the casualty rate was enormous, there were still more soldiers coming forward to man the front lines. The German chiefs of staff declared: 'We estimated that we should have to contend with 180 Russian divisions; we have already counted 360.'

The third trump was the productivity of Russian industry which, through patriotic fervour and an astonishing rebirth of effort, kept its men at war supplied with arms and machines, outstripping the manufacture of German goods.

In the factories, on the farms and cities and on the front line, it would be a long and arduous grind to victory for the people of the Soviet Union. Hitler sent in special task forces called the Einsatzgruppen which massacred Jews, Communists, gypsies and other so-called undesirables en route through Russia. Civilians who escaped ill-treatment from the Germans had their own countrymen to fear. The NKVD slaughtered scores in the prisons of towns like Lvov before they fell to the Germans.

As the Red Army became more effective under the leadership of outstanding generals like Georgy Zhukov, so the balance of the war changed. A failed Soviet offensive in the spring of 1942 was followed by a major German offensive in the south aiming to seize the oilfields of the Caucuses that culminated in the fierce battle for Stalingrad – the first major German surrender of World War II and perhaps the Red Army's greatest victory. The Germans in the spring of 1943 attacked the town of Kursk, fought the largest tank battle in history and were badly beaten by a well-prepared enemy.

A push by the Red Army forced the Germans back to the Polish border in August 1944. For the first time in the war, the conflict was being carried into Third Reich territory. As a bonus, thousands of German troops had been tied up on the eastern front, enabling the Allies to execute the D-Day landings on the beaches of Normandy in June 1944 and to begin the liberation of Western Europe.

On the Eastern Front, the retreat of the German forces was remorseless. By April 1945, units of the Red Army were fighting their way house by house through the streets of Berlin. On 30 April, Hitler shot himself in his bunker beneath the city. On May 2, Russian soldiers raised their flag atop the Reichstag building – an iconic image that became a symbol of the Soviet victory over Nazi Germany.

The 'Big Three' conference in Teheran in November 1943, attended by Stalin, Roosevelt and Churchill.

The 'Big Three' meet again, at Yalta, in the Crimea, in February 1945.

The Red Flag is raised over the Reichstag on 2 May 1945.

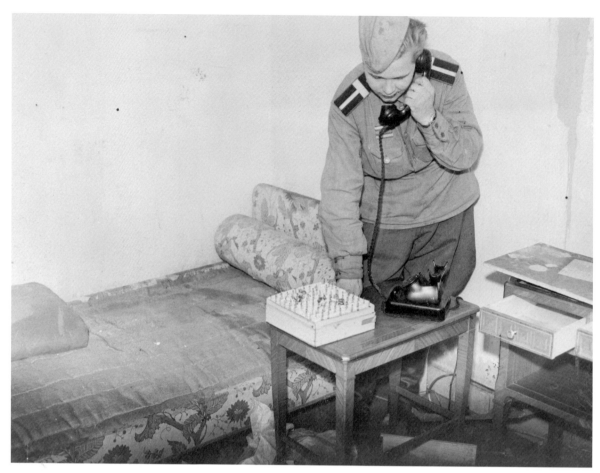

Inside Hitler's bunker… A Russian
soldier tries the telephone in Eva
Braun's bedroom. The box on her
bedside table contains phials of poison.

A Red Army soldier carries off a
souvenir of the battle for Berlin: a
bust of the dead Führer.

German commanders who had defended Berlin sign their surrender in May 1945.

Despite having only narrowly snatched victory from the jaws of seemingly certain defeat, Stalin portrayed himself as a military genius.

The image of Stalin the conqueror peers down on a Victory Parade in Red Square on 24 June 1945

The new leader of the Free World is introduced to Stalin for the first time… Harry S. Truman, who became US President following the death of F.D. Roosevelt, meets the Soviet leader in Potsdam, Germany, in July 1945 to discuss the post-war pattern of European borders. Also at the conference was Winston Churchill – replaced midway by newly elected British Prime Minister Clement Attlee.

The conference is most noted for the strongly anti-Communist stance of Truman, who famously said: 'The Russians only understand one language – how many armies have you got?'

At Potsdam, Truman's strongest bargaining chip was his ominous announcement that the US had just detonated the first atomic bomb. Stalin appeared unimpressed; thanks to his intelligence network, he already knew.

Stalin in the ultimate seat of power… Coolly confident, cigarette in hand, he was the one
leader among the 'Big Three' at Potsdam who held most of the bargaining chips when it
came to carving up Europe following the defeat of the Third Reich.

Display of power… Victory Day in Red Square in 1946.

A wave to the crowds in Red Square.

The toll of World War II on the Soviet people was 20 million, a loss far greater than any other nation. Yet Stalin was the acclaimed hero of the hour. He accepted the title of 'Generalissimus'. At summit conferences of the war leaders, he rubbed shoulders with Britain's Winston Churchill and American President Franklin D. Roosevelt, international heavyweights who were poles apart from him ideologically but united in their aim of smashing Hitler. Together the trio planned a new world order to follow the ending of hostilities. Stalin revelled in his new image of wise elder statesman.

Sadly, the ties that bound the three nations together in times of strife were not strong enough to survive the ravages of peace.

* * *

At the end of the war, the German country and its capital Berlin were divided into four sectors. They fell under the control of the victorious nations Britain, the United States, France and the Soviet Union. Even before the war was over, the Allies had agreed to seek reparations from Germany and each zone was to provide compensation to its occupying country. Stalin took full advantage of the agreement. Complete factories were dismantled and transported to the USSR, along with key workers. Stalin was determined to wring as much as possible out of the vanquished Germany, to the consternation of the rest of the Allies.

Stalin had been courteous towards Churchill and Roosevelt and probably held them in a high regard. But before the end of the war Churchill had been replaced as British premier by Clement Atlee in a general election and Roosevelt had died. His successor Harry Truman was less accommodating towards Stalin. Although Britain, America and France had during wartime paved the way for the unforeseen Russian domination of Eastern Europe, the victorious countries were now unhappy about the arrangement.

For his part, Stalin became increasingly suspicious; his prewar paranoia had returned. He was convinced that the Western Allies had dragged their feet in the conflict in order that Germany and Russia fought each other for as long as possible in the hope that both would be destroyed. He threw a cloak of secrecy over Eastern Europe.

Gradually, the presence of British, American and French troops was withdrawn and Germans were handed back the western part of their country. Stalin, however, was determined to stay put. He was unwilling to relinquish the empire that had been built in Germany, the Baltic states and east European countries.

On a visit to the USA in 1946, Winston Churchill spoke prophetically about the seriously deteriorating relations with Stalin: 'Nobody knows what Soviet Russia and its Communist International organisation intends to do in the immediate future or what are the limits, if any, of their expansive and proselytising tendencies. From Stettin on the Baltic to Trieste on the Adriatic, an iron curtain has descended across the continent.'

As far back as the 1920s, Stalin had determined that the Soviet Union's immediate neighbours should be countries with Communist regimes. Gradually, Communist governments took power in those countries of Eastern Europe: Poland and Romania in 1947, followed by Bulgaria, Czechoslovakia and Hungary in 1948.

The Soviet troops who had liberated these countries from Nazism now in their turn became oppressors. People who had fled before the arrival of the Soviet troops were handed back to face unknown horrors. Red Army soldiers who had been prisoners of war in German territories were likewise transported into Russia. In Stalin's eyes, they were guilty of cowardice and betrayal. Many were executed without trial. The remainder were mostly worked to death.

Worse was to come. A US aid plan devised by Secretary of State George Marshall in 1948 injected west European countries with food, fuel, raw materials and machinery. Stalin viewed it as American expansionism of the worst order. It was the same year that the western countries decided to unite the divided zones of Germany. Russia's response was to isolate allied West Berlin in the heart of the Soviet zone. For a year the Western countries airlifted supplies to the sector. Even when the stalemate was broken, West Berlin remained an 'island' in the midst of the Communist world.

And that world was by now an empire. Added to the Soviet Union at the end of World War II were parts of Finland, Romania and Czechoslovakia, half of Poland and East Prussia, plus the Baltic States. He had also established sympathetic buffer states in the rest of Czechoslovakia, in Hungary, Bulgaria and Romania. Also, by entering the war against Japan at the last moment, Stalin had 'legitimised' the annexation of the Kurile Islands, Sakhalin Island and parts of Mongolia. His sinister rule now stretched from the

A grim pose… This is the man who believed that 'one death is a tragedy, one million is a statistic'.

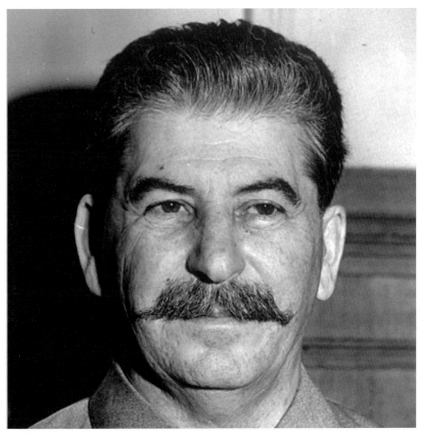

Steely-eyed Stalin, who once said: 'I believe in one thing only – the power of the human will.'

Sea of Japan to the River Elbe in Germany. And just as Hitler's Propaganda Minister Joseph Goebbels had predicted in the dying days of Nazi Germany, mass butchery began within those heavily fortified borders.

At home, life for the victorious Soviet people was horrific. There was a woeful shortage of housing, severe rationing and Draconian working conditions. There were uprisings among the cold and hungry, each one ruthlessly suppressed. Communist ideals like collectivisation were once again enforced with a vengeance. The result was a famine in the Ukraine. Party chief of the region Nikita Khrushchev, a future Soviet leader, made a personal plea to Stalin. He received a characteristically brutish reply. 'You're being soft-bellied!' Khrushchev was told. 'They are deceiving you. They are counting on being able to appeal to your sentimentality.'

The Gulag camps were again filled with prisoners as the NKVD relaunched their purges. Whole peoples suspected of having collaborated with the Nazis – Chechens,

Grinning widely, Stalin was not noted for his humour, although he once bafflingly asserted that 'gaiety is the most outstanding feature of the Soviet Union.'

Stalin and his successor Nikita Khrushchev acknowledge the crowds in Red Square.

the Crimean Tartars, Kalmyks and Karachi-Balkars – were transported to starvation in Central Asia and Siberia. Returning soldiers who had witnessed too much of Western life were interrogated and shot.

In Leningrad, the heroic city that had suffered so badly during the war, there was a purge by party chief Andrei Zhdanov against intellectuals, artists and poets. Composers Shostakovich and Prokofiev were under fire for not writing tunes which could be whistled by a worker. Stalin viewed such activities with approval – until he realised that Zhdanov was creating a power base of his own. Although Zhdanov died of natural causes, there followed a purge against the party officials in Leningrad. Unlike the pre-war purges, this one did not involve a show trial; those purged were shot out of hand.

Stalin was fearful of intrigue and conspiracy. His daughter Svetlana described her father as being 'as bitter as could be against the whole world. He saw enemies everywhere. It had reached the point of being pathological, of being persecution mania'.

Even in the Kremlin, Stalin wore a bullet-proof vest. He travelled in an armour-plated car with bullet-proof windows seven centimetres thick. His food came from a NKVD farm and was tested by bodyguards for poison before every meal. He did not even like appearing above ground; tunnels were dug to link his office with other government departments, and the Moscow underground was extended to his suburban villa at Kuntsevo. The man who had imposed Soviet slavery on free nations had also become a prisoner of his own terror.

In the last few years of his life, Stalin's anti-Semitism reached new heights. He unleashed a tide of retribution against Jews whom he saw as bourgeois nationalists and described as 'rootless cosmopolitans'. His addled brain then created another grotesque conspiracy. In January 1953 Moscow Radio announced that Kremlin doctors were plotting to murder the leaders of the country, Stalin included. The unfortunate doctors were branded 'killers in white coats' and were carted off to Moscow's notorious Lubyanka, headquarters of the secret police, for interrogation and certain death. The cauldron of anti-Semitism looked set to boil over. But in March 1953 Stalin's train of terror stopped in its tracks…

Stalin had left the Kremlin for his dacha outside Moscow for the last time in mid-February and had since been involved in nightly heavy drinking sessions. On 1 March his guards became alarmed that there had been no sound from his room all day and, nervously entering his quarters, found him lying unconscious on the floor of his bedroom. He had suffered a brain haemorrhage and fallen into a coma.

NKVD chief Beria was called but on his arrival shouted at the staff: 'Can't you see that Comrade Stalin is in a deep sleep. Get out of here and don't wake him up.' Khrushchev, Molotov and fellow party leaders Georgy Malenkov and Nikolai

Left and above: Palace of a despot... This grandiose dacha was Stalin's private residence near the former town of Kuntsevo, now part of greater Moscow. Built for him in 1934, he lived there for the last two decades of his life, dying on a sofa in his dining room on 5 March 1953.

Bulganin also visited the dacha but were told only that Stalin had been laid on a sofa in his dining room 'in an unpresentable state' and was still asleep. Not realising the seriousness of his condition and fearful of upsetting him, they returned to Moscow.

Not until the next day, 2 March, with Stalin paralysed and speechless, were doctors summoned and announced that he had suffered a stroke. The hierarchy of the Soviet Union also appeared to be suffering from a form of paralysis. Leading Politburo members visited the dacha every day and dithered, fearfully uncertain what to do, while rumours spread of a plot to put an end to the dictator.

During these days of inertia, Stalin was being slowly suffocated by a lack of oxygen and his brain gradually destroyed. His son Vasily appeared briefly and screamed at Beria: 'You bastards, you're killing my father.' It was something that the NKVD chief would happily have done but was too fearful to implement.

Stalin's daughter Svetlana was at his bedside on the evening of 5 March when her father's eyes opened and, realising his predicament, appeared to be 'full of the fear of death'. She later recalled: 'The last hours were nothing but a slow strangulation. The death agony was terrible. He literally choked to death as we watched. At the very last moment, he suddenly opened his eyes and cast a glance over everyone in the room. It was a terrible gaze – insane or perhaps angry. He lifted his left hand as if he was pointing to something and bringing down a curse on us all. The gesture was full of menace. The next moment he was gone.'

Stalin was declared dead at 9.50 pm on 5 March 1953. It was announced the following day to the people of Russia on Moscow Radio: 'The heart of Joseph Vissarionovich Stalin, Lenin's comrade-in-arms and the genius-endowed continuer of his work, has ceased to beat.'

For three days Stalin's body lay in state in the Hall of Columns. Hordes of people filed before it, six abreast. Soon they ceased to form lines and became a sea of struggling humanity. Before the doors closed there was a queue some seven miles long. Army lorries were brought in to form barriers but succeeded only in fatally compressing the mob. Amid the throng, variously reported as being up to a million strong, as many as 500 mourners died, crushed or trodden underfoot.

Stalin's body was embalmed and on 9 March his coffin was ceremonially taken to the renamed Lenin-Stalin Mausoleum on Red Square and there was a national ten minutes' silence. Those who mourned him felt he represented stability and order in their vast and disparate nation. It was accurately reported that even prisoners in the countless labour camps of the Gulag wept.

The Soviet Union was by this time the world's largest sovereign state – a federation of 15 union republics, with another 20 autonomous republics and several smaller provinces. It occupied an area of 22,500,000 square kilometres (8,650,000

Dictator at rest… Stalin lying in state in the Hall of Columns in Moscow's House of Unions.

square miles) from Iran to Finland, from Czechoslovakia to China. It was unwieldy and needed more than the bombast of a bully like Joseph Stalin to hold it together.

* * *

The personality cult of Stalinism crumbled astonishingly quickly after his death. He was succeeded as First Secretary of the Communist Party of the Soviet Union by Georgy Malenkov. A few days later Malenkov lost the secretaryship to Nikita Khrushchev, who hastily (and wisely) began dismantling Stalin's power base. Khrushchev had learned his lesson from his years of streetfighting – both with a gun in the early days of revolution and through sheer ambition in the corridors of the Kremlin. But the effect of his arrival was that collective leadership had returned to the Soviet Union.

The NKVD apparatus of fear, which had mushroomed to one and a half million men and women, was scaled down and renamed the KGB. Its reviled leaders were executed within months of Stalin's death. First to go was Laventi Beria, head of the secret police and a contender for leadership, who was arrested at a meeting of the Politburo, unceremoniously hauled into court for a brief trial and shot.

The masses of the USSR, fed information only through the official propaganda machine, were not immediately aware of the dramatic changes at their country's helm. They were not told of the barbaric excesses of the recently lauded Stalin. It was not until 1956, at the 20th Party Congress, that Khrushchev denounced the former hero for cruelty and oppression, for crimes against the party and for building a 'cult of personality'.

Yet even this was kept from the mass of Soviet citizenry. It received wider circulation among the foreign Communist parties. As news travelled across the world, many were stunned. Their loyalty to avuncular Stalin was beyond question. For years they had blamed the purges on secret police chiefs and the privations on industrial wreckers.

At the 1961 party congress, Stalin's reputation was further tarnished. He was branded as little more than a common criminal, with the regime he led accused of 'criminal violations of socialist legality'. They hauled down his statues and his preserved body was removed from the Lenin Mausoleum and buried by the Kremlin Wall, a demotion to the second rank of the Soviet pantheon.

Yet sadly the turn-about did not herald a new era of freedom. The Soviet people had to wait another 30 years for that … for glasnost, for the tearing down of the Iron Curtain and for the removal of further vestiges of Stalin's tyrannical regime.

And yet the idolatry that had once allowed this ogre to flourish was not yet buried. More than half a century after his death came signs that the steely veneer of Stalinism had not entirely lost its popular lustre and that the unquestioning adulation he once engendered was still eerily mirrored in the admiration of many twenty-first century Russians.

In a yearning for renewed national prestige – and a denial of the lessons of history – there are signs that the Stalin cult is being resurrected at the highest political levels, the evidence of his brutal rule being eclipsed by the legacy of his industrialisation of the USSR and his stand against the Nazis in what the Russians call 'the Great Patriotic War'. It is an attitude seemingly encouraged by the more hawkish of Russia's leaders who tend to honour Stalin for his defeat of Nazi Germany without mentioning his decades of murderous purges, catastrophic collectivisation and other repressive policies that led to the death of millions.

Marble museum in honour of Stalin. It was built over his birthplace in Gori in the 'Thirties on the orders of Lavrentiy Beria, then head of the Georgian Communist Party.

A Cold War statue of Stalin that reminded East Berliners who was really in charge of their destiny.

Sculptor Sergei Merkurov's heroic statue of Stalin made the 'Man of Steel' into a man of marble.

A frieze in a Mosco Metro station is typical of the Stalin personality cult.

After ex-KGB strongman Vladimir Putin rose to power in 1999, Russia became increasingly authoritarian and militaristic, making Stalin's dictatorship seem more palatable. Stalin-era rhetoric returned. Opposition figures were again branded 'enemies of the state' and non-governmental organisations labelled 'foreign agents'. Putin, when accused of presiding over the creeping rehabilitation of Stalin, harked back to his stand against the Nazis, remarking: 'Whatever anyone may say about him, victory was achieved.'

As popular recognition of this, Belarus's Stalin Line museum was opened outside Minsk in 2005 to mark the sixtieth anniversary of the end of the war in which 20 million Soviet soldiers and citizens died – ignoring the fact that the horrific toll was partly due to Stalin's own military incompetence. Visitors there watch reenactments of tank battles and the firing of Soviet-era weapons, then line up to be photographed in front of a wreath-draped monument honouring him.

Stalin's birthplace of Gori, which already has a Stalin museum in his honour, closed in 1989 with the collapse of the Soviet Union but has since reopened, with the town voting to erect a huge statue of the dictator. The planners realised that it would have to be taller than his actual height of about 5ft 5ins (1.65m) – which he tried to disguise with built-up shoes adding extra inches to his diminutive stature.

Other monuments to Stalin have been unveiled in cities east of Moscow. In Penza the Communist party moved a bust from its headquarters to the city centre, where a brave liberal politician complained: 'Today the Communists exalt Stalin, but if tomorrow they decide to erect busts of Pol Pot or Hitler would prosecutors remain as passive?' In Mari-El (statistically credited with being the 'suicide capital of the world') the Communist Party unveiled a 9ft statue as 'a tribute to a great man whose name has been unjustly forgotten for 60 years'.

Several surveys this century have shown that Stalin is more popular today than he was during the collapse of the Soviet Union in 1991. In 2008 a Russia-wide poll put him as the third most revered figure in its history – amid suspicion that the vote had been rigged to deprive him of being placed first. A 2013 survey found that 45 percent of Russians had a 'generally positive' view of him, with 60 percent agreeing with the statement that 'for all his mistakes and misdeeds, the most important thing is that under his leadership the Soviet people won the Great Patriotic War'. In Georgia, his home state, a poll found 68 percent agreeing that 'Stalin was a wise leader who brought the Soviet Union to might and prosperity.' An independent poll in 2015 revealed that 40 percent of Russians considered him 'more good than bad' and almost half believed the sacrifice of millions of lives under Stalin were justified given the speed of the Soviet Union's economic growth during his rule – a statistic that had almost doubled since an identical poll two years earlier.

Those last two surveys were conducted by the prestigious Washington-based Carnegie Endowment for International Peace, whose authors are troubled both by the high levels of regard for Stalin particularly among older citizens and the seeming indifference towards his transgressions by younger Russians – possibly because history textbooks published in the last few years tend to ignore Stalin's crimes. History teachers have even lost their jobs simply for speaking the truth about the Stalin years.

The Carnegie study points to the danger of allowing the Stalin cult to take root again because another Russian strongman might learn lessons from him and use his wartime victory and enforced national unity to validate the newly authoritarian political order. As the report warns, despite being buried in Moscow, 'Stalin is not dead'.

So while outside Russia's borders Joseph Stalin is listed alongside Adolf Hitler and China's Mao Zedong in terms of their brutality, his image within his own country is more opaque. History is being rewritten. The monster is being resurrected. It's a disturbing thought as the Russian bear again sharpens its claws.

Stalin as he would have wished to be remembered… a strong leader and father figure to his people. In truth, his view of them was cynically summed up thus: 'The way to handle people is to treat them like chickens. Take away everything they have by plucking all their feathers and then throw them a few breadcrumbs. They will then follow you forever.'

Principal Dates

1879   Stalin is born on 18 December.

1890   Enters Gori Theological School. Father dies.

1894   Enters Tbilisi Seminary.

1898   Joins Tbilisi Marxists.

1900   Finds work at Tbilisi Observatory.

1901   Loses job and goes underground.

1902   Arrested.

1903   Sentenced to three years' exile in Siberia in July.

1904   Escapes from Siberia in February and marries later that year.

1908   First son Yakov is born on 16 March. Stalin is arrested and imprisoned and by November he is in exile in Vologda.

1909   Escapes from exile. His first wife dies.

1910   Arrested at Baku and exiled.

1911   Completes exile and moves to St Petersburg, where he is arrested and exiled once more.

1912   Escapes from exile in March and is arrested in St Petersburg two months later and again exiled. He finally escapes in September.

1913   Adopts the name Stalin, meaning 'Man of Steel'. Previously known as Koba, meaning 'the indomitable'. Arrested in St Petersburg and exiled to the Arctic Circle.

1917   Rejected for army service as medically unfit. Works on Pravda, the Communist Party newspaper during the March revolution. In November he becomes Chairman for Nationalities.

1918   In charge of grain collection in southern Russia. Exacts grain from Tsaritsyn in the face of enemy action.

1919   Declines various posts to stay in Moscow and secure a power base.

1922   Lenin suffers his first stroke in May.

1923   Lenin threatens to break off relations with Stalin in March, shortly before the leader suffers his third stroke.

1924   Lenin dies on 21 January.

1925   Trotsky is removed as Commissar for War.

1928   Trotsky is exiled then expelled from the USSR.

1932   Stalin's second wife commits suicide.

1934   Kirov is assassinated.

1935   Show trial of Zinoviev, Kamenev and others. The terror begins.
1939   Non-Aggression Pact signed between USSR and Germany in August. World War II breaks out the following month.
1940   Trotsky is assassinated.
1941   Stalin replaces Molotov as Soviet Prime Minister in May. 'Operation Barbarossa' brings USSR into the war in June. Stalin appoints himself Commander in Chief of the Red Army.
1942   Red Army holds Wehrmacht at bay in Moscow.
1943   Stalingrad won by Red Army in February. Battle of Kursk won by Red Army in July. Stalin meets Roosevelt and Churchill at Tehran Conference.
1944   Leningrad siege over after 900 days. Red Army wins back much of Eastern Europe.
1945   Yalta Conference, with Stalin, Churchill and Roosevelt in February. Victory in Europe by May. Map of Europe is redrawn at Potsdam Conference by Stalin, Truman and Atlee. In August Stalin declares war on Japan, less than a month before it surrenders.
1948   Attempt to block food supplies reaching West Berlin fails when the US airlifts supplies into the city.
1952   Last major public speech made by Stalin at the 19th Congress of the Communist Party of the Soviet Union.
1953   Stalin dies on 5 March.